s'mores

s'mores

LISA ADAMS

Photographs by Susan Barnson Hayward

GIBBS SMITH
TO ENRICH AND INSPIRE HUMANKIND

Second Edition
24 23 22 21   5 4 3 2

Published by
Gibbs Smith
P.O. Box 667
Layton, Utah 84041

1.800.835.4993 orders
www.gibbs-smith.com

Designed by Sheryl Dickert
Printed and bound in China
Gibbs Smith books are printed on either recycled, 100% post-consumer waste,
FSC-certified papers or on paper produced from sustainable PEFC-certified forest/
controlled wood source. Learn more at www.pefc.org.

Library of Congress Cataloging-in-Publication Data

Names: Adams, Lisa, author. | Hayward, Susan Barnson, photographer.
Title: S'mores : gourmet treats for every occasion / Lisa Adams, photographs by
Susan Barnson Hayward.
Description: Second edition. | Layton, Utah : Gibbs Smith, [2020] | Includes index.
Identifiers: LCCN 2019028692 | ISBN 9781423654360 (hardcover) | ISBN
9781423654377 (epub)
Subjects: LCSH: Desserts. | Cooking (Marshmallow) | LCGFT: Cookbooks.
Classification: LCC TX799 .A33 2020 | DDC 641.8/53—dc23
LC record available at https://lccn.loc.gov/2019028692

For my family, all of you.

contents

acknowledgments

This book would not exist without the contributions of many, many hungry people.

I owe the very concept to Neva Healer and Bonnie Steward—and the lure of a particularly succulent strawberry on a momentous May night. They and everyone in my Rock Creek family—a hardy and numerous bunch—were there from the very beginning as invaluable collaborators and taste-testers.

I must also thank the Superfriends for their eager sampling, silly recipe names, and help with new recipes for this second edition. They, along with my Ninjas, have championed this book for over a decade now, enthusiastically spreading the word without a great deal of begging on my part. I am all the more grateful knowing how rare this kind of support actually is. Thank you for being the best friends.

Most of the "hard" work of fine-tuning these recipes happened at home, and so I owe a thousand thanks to John, Emma, and Alexis Heath, who ate whatever I made and endured my endless hours of pondering and tweaking. I trust that no other family has consumed so many s'mores in their own kitchen.

Much has been said about soulmates, but rarely do the poets enumerate what one might do to help the other complete a jaunty dessert cookbook. The answer is *everything*, from opining on recipes to becoming a food stylist for a week. (Sure, it could have been worse, but I'm certain that my stupendous husband would have been *almost* as instrumental had my book featured kale or cauliflower. Probably.)

I'm grateful to everyone at Gibbs Smith for believing in this book and keeping the magic alive for another edition. It's been wonderful to relive the experience with my daughter Alexis, who wasn't yet born the first time around—and honestly had no idea that her mother was the S'more Queen.

I am indebted to each and every one of you for making this book happen. S'mores would still be boring if it were not for you!

introduction

I've been eating s'mores my whole life, and I have to tell you—they didn't used to be very interesting.

Call me a literalist, but it should be nearly impossible to stop eating something called "some more." Yet consistently I found myself brushing s'mores aside to stuff my face with other delectable treats, like cake and ice cream and candy.

It didn't seem right. So I set out to invent s'mores that really lived up to their name.

When I wrote the first edition of this book in 2005, the very concept of fancy s'mores, or even a "s'more recipe," did not exist in the public consciousness. I searched libraries and Google, and while I found hundreds of recipes for s'more-inspired pies, cakes, and cookies, I didn't find a single reference to constructing a s'more with anything but milk chocolate and graham crackers.

Luckily, Gibbs Smith agreed with me that s'mores deserved better, and in 2007 they published my book *S'mores: Gourmet Treats for Every Occasion*—the first cookbook on s'mores in the world. I was interviewed by dozens of newspapers and radio stations in the years that followed, and pretty quickly the idea started catching on. Today, you'll find embellished s'mores everywhere—online, in restaurants, on cooking channels, and even at a friend's barbecue or birthday party.

Whether or not you've delved into this brave new world before, in this book you'll find unbelievably delicious recipes that may just change the way you think about s'mores. Using chocolates, fruits, and bakery treats of every variety, these recipes are designed to enhance the treat we know and love, bringing a little more variety, creativity, and fun to the fire. Whether you make s'mores at home or out in nature, I hope these variations make you melt with delight and reinvigorate your love for this venerable dessert sandwich.

what is a s'more?

t's a good question. Until recently, the definition was pretty obvious: a s'more was a dessert sandwich made from a graham cracker, a piece of chocolate, and a roasted marshmallow. That recipe has been around forever—or at least since 1927, when it was first published in a Girl Scout handbook.

I set out to expand that definition. But as I began to enter uncharted s'more territory, I was left with an unanswered question: What *does* make a s'more a s'more?

After consulting several oracles, I made a decision: while many of the s'more recipes in this book do not contain graham crackers, and a few don't have chocolate, every recipe contains a roasted marshmallow. If you don't like marshmallows, or don't eat gelatin, you can omit the marshmallow from almost all the recipes and still have a delicious dessert (s'mores are flexible that way). But in expanding the concept, I felt that there had to be at least one common ingredient that linked these recipes to their noble ancestor. The marshmallow, roasted over a campfire, has always been the essence of s'mores—despite the new recipes and new cooking methods, the marshmallow remains the foundation, and the heart, of this beloved dessert sandwich.

how to make s'mores

t's not just a matter of adding new ingredients. That's a big part of it, of course, but the real key to phenomenal s'mores is melting those ingredients. And that's a step that needs some explaining.

Though we all associate s'mores with campfires, you can make the recipes in this book without exposing even a fingernail to the wilderness. Barbecues, fireplaces, home s'more makers, ovens, and stovetops can deliver the same goods as a stick and a fire pit. Whatever your preferred cooking arrangement, here are all the tips and tricks you'll need to make sublime s'mores.

CHOOSING YOUR INGREDIENTS

If you're going to make a specific s'more for a specific occasion, pick your recipe and buy the ingredients. Voilà!

For parties and camping trips, however, I'd highly recommend the Buffet Experience. It can be momentous, even life-changing—especially for those who never dreamed such a thing could exist. Imagine surprising your hardened, unsuspecting campfire cronies with an eye-popping spread of chocolates, sliced fruits, and outrageous toppings, bathed in the flickering light of a propane lantern. Your friends are guaranteed to love you forever and might very well cry with joy.

The best way to plan your buffet is to flip through this book, note the recipes you'd most like to try, and make a list of ingredients. Your budget may dictate how much you buy, but I'd recommend choosing enough ingredients to make at least a few different kinds of s'mores. Be sure to consider the melting factor when purchasing your chocolates—it's very tempting to save some money by grabbing those giant, thick versions of your favorite candy bars, but keep in mind that if you like melted chocolate, you will have difficulty with these monster-size treats. On the other hand, some people prefer their chocolate unmelted, so there's no harm in stocking up on both slender and substantial candy bars when choosing your chocolate.

When it comes to marshmallows, the best roasters tend to be your standard store-bought varieties. In addition to the regular white puff, in some grocery stores you can also find flavored choices, as well as marshmallows coated in toasted coconut (which pair deliciously with melted caramel in the Toasted Coconut Caramel Recipe [page 73]).

Many specialty food stores and candy shops (and their websites) sell handmade marshmallows in all sorts of luscious fruit and confectionary flavors, such as raspberry, banana, caramel, and mint-chocolate. These confections are usually cube-shaped and larger than standard marshmallows. Their shape and size can make them difficult to roast thoroughly, so I like to cut them in half before roasting or use a metal cooking rod to ensure the centers liquefy. Because these specialty marshmallows can be expensive and hard to find, I have not used them in many of my recipes—but if you have them, feel free to use them in place of regular marshmallows. In the Resources section [page 124], you'll find a list of some places to buy them.

As for graham crackers, use any kind you like. The cinnamon and chocolate varieties taste almost identical to regular honey grahams when used in s'mores, and their appearance lends well to fancier presentations. For an extra bit of chocolate, you can also try topping your s'mores with chocolate-dipped graham crackers instead of plain ones.

YOU'RE GOING TO TAKE ALL THAT CAMPING?

Folks today have numerous and conflicting ideas about what camping is and should be. Clearly some campers must eat nothing but oatmeal and ramen noodles, because after hearing about some of my recipes, a few people have looked at me blankly and asked, "You're going to take all that *camping?*" Well, sure—some of my camping friends eat better around the fire than I do at home! We all believe in eating well in the woods, and that includes great s'mores.

While some of the recipes in this book may be too much for the "oatmeal and ramen" type of camper, almost everyone should be able to make several s'more varieties using ingredients that they would normally bring on any camping trip. Some of the easiest and tastiest s'mores contain nothing more exotic than fresh or dried fruit. It's also easy to replace plain milk chocolate with your favorite candy bar, or graham crackers with cookies. So don't worry—s'mores are for everyone!

SETTING UP YOUR BUFFET

Once you're ready to make a night of it, pick a convenient spot and arrange your ingredients. It usually works best to use a well-lit table a short distance from the fire so that buffet visitors can choose their ingredients without tripping over roasters and sticks. Using a table also keeps the ingredients orderly and out of the grime. (You *can* stash ingredients in different people's laps around the fire, but this lazy arrangement often leads to common s'more afflictions, such as the Unspeakably Broken Grahams, the Suspiciously Vanishing Chocolate Bar, and the dreaded Dirt-Encrusted Marshmallow Bag.)

If all this sounds too cumbersome, just make s'mores indoors or during the day. Sure, you'll lose some atmosphere, but you'll also eliminate many of the challenges that can besiege a customary campfire arrangement.

COOKING YOUR S'MORES

One of the biggest and most disappointing lies I've ever heard was that a roasted marshmallow will melt a piece of chocolate. Unless the chocolate

is *very* thin and the marshmallow *very* hot, it just doesn't happen. It's a crime, and so I offer a lot of melting tips in this book. While s'mores are still tasty with unmelted chocolate (I mean, hey, it's *choco-late*), I believe that the meltiness of a s'more is just as important as its exciting ingredients. There's even an economic advantage, since you'll need a lot less chocolate if you melt it—1/4 or less of a full-size candy bar per s'more. So I'll go through the melting techniques for each heat source—fire, barbecue grill, oven, fireplace, s'more kit/stovetop, and micro-wave—to set you on the course to truly gooey treats.

FRIENDLY FIRE

If you are cooking s'mores over a wood fire, it's preferable to wait until the flames have produced a good quantity of glowing embers. You'll have more heat and more control when cooking over these coals—both for roasting marshmallows and melting chocolate.

The good news is that you don't need a perfect fire to make fantastic s'mores. Most of the fires I use are a mix of flame and embers, flickering in a metal pit with a partially adjustable cooking grate. I simply work with what I have, trying to keep the flames and coal beds apart as much as possible. Then I follow the guidelines below.

If your fire does not have soaring flames, you can place your graham cracker (with chocolate and other ingredients on top) directly on the grate, and then simply pluck it off quickly when the ingredients have melted. Obviously, the farther away from the coals, the longer the melting process will take. For this reason, I recommend using a bottom graham cracker (or sturdy cookie, like shortbread) for most s'mores; grahams will not fall apart even if stuck on a grill for a long time (though they *will* burn if abandoned for an extended period).

If your fire *does* have soaring flames, you can use a frying pan to melt your ingredients. Put the chocolate-laden graham cracker into the pan, and put the pan on the grate. When the ingredients have melted properly, you can take the pan off the grate and slide the graham onto a plate with a spatula. For best results, do this last step at a decently lit table. If you have no table available, have someone else hold your plate so you don't accidentally cast your just-melted delight into the night. Though it can be a bit unwieldy, the pan process can cook several s'mo-res at once and melt the ingredients consistently. It also prevents grahams from getting burned. Don't use a fancy pan, though; the bottom can really get scorched.

You can also melt your ingredients by enclosing them in a package of heavy-duty aluminum foil. Tear off two same-size pieces of foil (about a foot-and-a-half square should be plenty) and place one directly on top of the other. Lay the graham cracker and ingredients in the middle, and fold up all four sides so that your graham cracker rests at the bottom of the packet. Then roll or pinch the foil together at the top to seal it. (It doesn't have to be pretty.) Set the foil package on the grate or, if you have no flames, close to the coals. When done, use tongs or a potholder to remove the package from the heat. Open it up (it will cool off in just a minute) and slide the s'more onto your plate. This method melts the ingredients well and is often the best process to use if you are not using a graham cracker for your bottom piece. But graham crackers and cookies can still burn this way, so don't leave the foil near the coals for too long.

Finally, if you don't want to mess with any extra equipment, use this shortcut: roast your marshmallow as usual. Once it's hot and melty, slide it on to your graham cracker. Then take your chocolate (thinner works better) and insert it *inside* the hot marshmallow. The liquid core of the marshmallow does a much better job melting the chocolate than the crusty outside layer. Top your s'more and enjoy.

Obviously, these melting methods require interaction with hot fires and grills, so they should not be attempted by those too young or imprudent to pull them off without getting hurt. While melting the chocolate is more challenging than standard s'more assembly, the extra step—whichever one you choose—will definitely be worth it!

BARBECUED S'MORES

Use your barbecue grill to make heavenly s'mores anytime the mood strikes. The real advantage of s'moring on a grill is that you can use the lid to ensure quick and thorough melting of your ingredients. I don't even roast my marshmallow—I just set it on top of my bottom graham cracker and leave the whole thing under the lid for a few minutes. The marshmallow doesn't turn golden brown, but it does melt over the rest of the ingredients and it tastes delicious.

Depending on the kind of grill you have, you may also be able to roast a marshmallow close to the heat while you melt ingredients on the grate. Without a lid, though, your ingredients will take longer to

melt, so make sure your graham cracker doesn't burn in the process.

BAKED S'MORES

If you're making s'mores for a large group, the oven is a great way to go. Just grab a baking sheet, line it with aluminum foil or parchment paper (for easy cleanup), and assemble your s'mores, omitting the top graham cracker (or alternative). Then pop the sheet into a preheated 350-degree oven for 4–6 minutes (oven temperatures vary, so make adjustments as needed). Your marshmallows, while not officially roasted, will puff up and melt over the ingredients. All you need to do, after cooling the s'mores for a minute or two, is add any final toppings.

It's best not to make particularly tall s'mores using this method; marshmallows can melt in unpredictable ways and are liable to plummet off a tower of ingredients. I'd recommend leaving off any fruit or anything else that doesn't need to be melted. Once the cooking is complete, you can squish these ingredients into your melted marshmallow. If you are making a s'more without graham crackers and need to heat both pieces (cookies, for example), just put the top piece next to the rest of the s'more on the baking sheet. Then, when everything is ready to go, complete the sandwich.

Whether you're making one signature s'more recipe for all your guests or giving each person free reign over a buffet, the oven method allows everyone to cook and enjoy their s'mores at once.

WHERE THE HEARTH IS

S'mores are also fun to make in a fireplace on a wintery evening at home. You probably won't have a cooking grate, but you can use the aluminum foil method described on page 17 to melt your ingredients while you roast marshmallows over coals or flames.

S'MORE KITS AND STOVETOPS

Home s'more-making kits are now available in stores and online. These usually consist of a ceramic burner and tray, outfitted with a grill, metal roasting forks, and a metal pot to hold the fuel.

There are many different kinds, so I can't review them all, but just be aware that they are often designed only for marshmallow-roasting—that is, there's no way to melt the chocolate with the device—and the fuel can burn marshmallows easily. Instead of using a kit, I simply use my gas stove. I roast my marshmallow by the flame of one burner

general principles to keep in mind

- Coals cook faster and more consistently than flames.

- Marshmallows cook faster on a metal cooking rod or coat hanger than on a stick or wooden rod.

- The more ingredients you use at once, the longer they will take to melt.

- The farther away from the heat source your ingredients are, the longer they will take to melt. (Okay, I know this one is obvious, but it still has to be part of your mental calculation.)

Therefore, if you are roasting marshmallows over coals but melting ingredients over a built-in grate a foot above the fire, you'll need to start melting those ingredients several minutes before you begin roasting the marshmallow. Again, you'll have to assess your individual situation each time, but it's not hard to get a basic idea of what will work and try it out. And even if you don't achieve perfection, the results will be tasty no matter what.

while melting ingredients in a frying pan over a second burner. I use low heat for melting ingredients and medium to medium-low for marshmallow-roasting—but every stove is different, so adjust your settings as needed.

MICROWAVE

If you want a s'more fast, the microwave is for you! It takes just 7–10 seconds to "roast" a marshmallow or melt ingredients in the microwave. The marshmallows will not really be roasted, of course, and they will lack the slightly crisp texture of their golden-brown cousins, but they will be puffy, soft, and just fine for a quick treat. (Don't heat marshmallows longer than 10 seconds or they will get immensely sticky and rubbery.)

OTHER COOKING TIPS

ROASTING MARSHMALLOWS

Some people like their marshmallows raw, others burned, but the consensus seems to be that golden brown works best. Creating these treats takes patience. The perfect soft, unscalded marshmallow comes from steady rotation near a heat source, ideally a bed of coals. For the most even roast, use a metal cooking rod or coat hanger and a steady hand. Regular ol' sticks are fine too, though they tend to be curved or kinky, which can make marshmallows cook unevenly. Metal devices will cook marshmallows faster than wooden ones and are more likely to deliver gooey centers.

TIMING

Ideally, you want your ingredients to be melted at exactly the same time your marshmallow finishes roasting. To accomplish this feat, you must assess your heat source and cooking setup and adjust your timing accordingly. It's a good idea to do a tester s'more or two to figure out how long roasting and melting will take before you begin heavy production.

DIVISION OF LABOR

Especially in a campfire setting, the whole procedure seems to work best when one person handles the marshmallow roasting and everyone else can worry about assembling and melting the contents of their own s'mores. Things can get a bit hairy when you're trying to hold a plate, a pan, a spatula, and a stick at the same time.

Fortunately for me, my brother Dustin is a world-class marshmallow roaster, and we all let him handle that portion of the proceedings entirely. His standards are so high that he will destroy a marshmallow if it isn't perfectly golden and melty, even at the protests of hungry friends. I know some people like to do it all themselves, but I personally like to concentrate on my ingredients, knowing that one of Dustin's perfect marshmallows will soon be melting upon them.

MAKING YOUR OWN RECIPES

In this book I've offered you many recipes beloved by friends and family, but the boundaries of my imagination shouldn't limit your experience. I encourage you to invent your own recipes, but there is a bit of danger in this (especially in conjunction with a buffet), as many people try to fit every kind of chocolate and topping on one s'more. Usually this approach is more stimulating to the eyes than to the palate; overloading a s'more with too many flavors tends to cancel them out. In general, it's much better to keep it simple—try one kind of new chocolate with one or *maybe* two additions. People get distressed at the thought that they won't be able to try everything, but it helps to keep faith that there will be another opportunity and another buffet in the future.

sweet starts

fruit flavor burst

Milk chocolate, to taste

1 graham cracker,
broken in half

1 marshmallow

1 slice strawberry, peach, or
mango, about $1/2$–1 inch thick

Arrange chocolate on 1 of the graham cracker halves and melt. Roast the marshmallow. Once the chocolate has melted, remove graham cracker from heat and layer with fruit and roasted marshmallow. Top with remaining graham cracker half.

Note: The best way to make this s'more is to use 1 fruit slice of uniform thickness that will cover as much of the graham cracker as possible. If you don't mind a messier eating experience, you can use several thinner slices of fruit instead (which may slide out when you take a bite). However you slice it, choose the juiciest and most flavorful fruit for the best possible s'more.

milky way melt

4 Milky Way Mini candy bars,
regular or dark chocolate

1 graham cracker,
broken in half

1 marshmallow

Distribute Milky Way Minis evenly on 1 of the graham cracker halves and melt. Because the chocolate is thinner than a standard chocolate bar, you won't need to heat your s'more as long as usual. Roast the marshmallow. When candy bar pieces have softened, remove graham cracker from heat, add roasted marshmallow and top with remaining graham cracker half.

VARIATIONS You can make this s'more with a graham cracker-size piece of a standard Milky Way bar. I prefer the Minis because they are easier to spread evenly over the graham cracker, and I like mixing the light and dark varieties in the same s'more. But the essential flavor can be achieved either way.

If you don't want quite so much nougat, you can use 2 Milky Way Minis and fill in the rest of the graham cracker with regular chocolate bar pieces.

simple mint

3 to 4 Andes mints

1/2 graham cracker

1 marshmallow

1 crispy mint cookie (Thin Mint, Mint Oreo, etc.)

Unwrap mints and melt them on the graham cracker. Roast the marshmallow. Once the chocolate has melted, remove graham cracker from heat and top with roasted marshmallow and mint cookie.

Note: The Andes mint is the nobility of the mint world. With its creamy consistency, high meltability, and luscious flavor, the Andes mint can be incorporated into almost any s'more for unbelievable results. That said, any chocolate filled or flavored with mint can be used in this recipe.

chocolate shortbread shortcut

1 marshmallow

2 Petit Écolier cookies,
or a similar cookie

Roast the marshmallow, ensuring it is heated all the way through. Sandwich between 2 Petit Écolier cookies and give chocolate a moment to melt.

Thanks to Kate Kelsey and Bryan Zimmer for this handy shortcut.

sugar cookie crunch

$1/4$ full-size Nestlé Crunch White candy bar

2 sugar cookies

1 marshmallow

Arrange chocolate on 1 sugar cookie and melt. Keep heat low and watch carefully—sugar cookies can burn quickly! Roast the marshmallow. Once the chocolate has melted, remove cookie from heat and top with roasted marshmallow and remaining cookie.

simple orange

Orange-flavored
chocolate, to taste

$1/2$ graham cracker

1 marshmallow

1 Pim's orange biscuit

Arrange chocolate on the graham cracker and melt. Roast the marshmallow. Once the chocolate has melted, remove graham cracker from heat and top with roasted marshmallow and orange biscuit.

melon refresher

1 slice chilled cantaloupe, cut
to fit on a graham cracker half

Milk chocolate, to taste

1 graham cracker,
broken in half

1 marshmallow

At least an hour before roasting begins, cut a slice of cantaloupe (thickness is up to you, but try to use 1 piece rather than several slices) and wedge it next to something icy in the cooler (or, if you're at home, just pop it in the fridge). When it's time to make the s'more, arrange chocolate on 1 of the graham cracker halves and melt. Roast the marshmallow. Once the chocolate has melted, remove graham cracker from heat. Place chilled melon over chocolate and top with the roasted marshmallow and remaining graham cracker half.

chewy apricot

Dark chocolate, to taste

1 graham cracker,
broken in half

1 marshmallow

2 to 3 dried apricots

Arrange chocolate on 1 of the graham cracker halves and melt. Roast the marshmallow. Once chocolate has melted, remove graham cracker from heat and secure apricots in chocolate. Top with roasted marshmallow and remaining graham cracker half.

rocky road

Milk chocolate with
almonds, to taste

1 graham cracker,
broken in half

1 marshmallow

Arrange chocolate on 1 of the graham cracker halves and melt. Roast the marshmallow. Once the chocolate has melted, remove graham cracker from heat and top with roasted marshmallow and remaining graham cracker half.

VARIATION If you're out of nutty chocolate, try sprinkling chopped almonds onto the melted milk chocolate.

salty-sweet crunch

Milk or dark chocolate,
to taste

1 graham cracker,
broken in half

2 to 3 pretzels or potato chips

Arrange chocolate on 1 of the graham cracker halves and melt. Roast the marshmallow. Once the chocolate has melted, remove graham cracker from heat and affix pretzels or potato chips in the melted chocolate. Top with remaining graham cracker half.

cornflake crisp

Milk chocolate, to taste

1 graham cracker,
broken in half

1 marshmallow

Cornflakes (or a crispy cereal
of your choice), to taste

Arrange chocolate on 1 of the graham cracker halves and melt. Roast the marshmallow. Once the chocolate has melted, remove graham cracker from heat and sprinkle cornflakes over chocolate. Top with roasted marshmallow and remaining graham cracker half.

VARIATION You can also use a chocolate bar already filled with cornflakes—the flakes will stay crisp even as the chocolate melts. See the Resources section (page 124) for a list of specialty chocolate brands.

the chocoholic

Milk or dark chocolate, to taste

2 large soft dark chocolate cookies

1 marshmallow, chocolate or regular

Arrange chocolate on 1 cookie and melt. If necessary, place second cookie over heat to soften. Roast the marshmallow. Once the chocolate has melted, remove cookie from heat and top with roasted marshmallow and remaining cookie.

the antioxidant

Dark chocolate, to taste

1 graham cracker, broken in half

1 marshmallow

5 to 10 fresh blueberries

Arrange chocolate on 1 of the graham cracker halves and melt. Roast the marshmallow. Once the chocolate has melted, remove graham cracker from heat and place fresh blueberries on chocolate, tapping to secure. Top with roasted marshmallow and remaining graham cracker half.

Thanks to Leigh Ann Gessner for this scrumptious recipe.

banana caramel

2 to 3 Hershey's Caramel Kisses, or any caramel-filled chocolate

1 graham cracker, broken in half

1 marshmallow

4 banana slices

Arrange Kisses on 1 of the graham cracker halves and melt. The chocolate is properly melted when it becomes soft and shiny—take care that you do not over-melt the chocolate, as the caramel filling can escape and spill. Roast the marshmallow. Once the chocolate has melted, remove graham cracker from heat and add sliced bananas, pressing them into the chocolate carefully. Add roasted marshmallow and top with remaining graham cracker half.

VARIATIONS Omit Kisses and use plain milk chocolate or milk chocolate with almonds. Top the chocolate and bananas with caramel syrup before adding the roasted marshmallow.

the fluffernutter

1 full-size Reese's Peanut
Butter Cup, or 2 to 3 minis

1 graham cracker,
broken in half

1 marshmallow

Place peanut butter cup on 1 of the graham cracker halves and melt. Roast the marshmallow. Once the chocolate has melted, remove graham cracker from heat and top with roasted marshmallow and remaining graham cracker half.

VARIATION Add four slices of banana. For stability's sake, your best bet is to place the banana slices on the graham cracker then add the peanut butter cup(s) on top of that—though this arrangement will take longer to melt the chocolate. You can add the bananas on top of the peanut butter cup(s) after melting, but take care not to lose the bananas as you take a bite!

the two-tone

2 distinct fruits, chocolates,
or candy toppings of choice*

1 graham cracker,
broken in half

1 marshmallow

This recipe is all about contrast: experiment with flavor, texture, or temperature by choosing one distinct topping for each half of your s'more.

Arrange 2 toppings of choice on 1 of the graham cracker halves and melt if desired. You can either swirl the 2 toppings together, or keep them completely separate for different taste and texture combinations. Roast the marshmallow. Once both components are ready, top with the roasted marshmallow. Finish off with the remaining graham cracker half.

*TASTY TOPPING COMBINATIONS
White and dark chocolate
Melted and unmelted chocolate
Melted chocolate and chilled fruit
Strawberries and bananas
Caramel and chocolate
Orange and white chocolate
Peaches and blackberries
Dried and fresh fruit
Lavender and white chocolate

dessert favorites

cookie dough

1 marshmallow

2 soft chocolate chip cookies

Chocolate chip cookie dough (homemade or store-bought), to taste

Roast the marshmallow and warm the cookies to soften, if desired. Spread a layer of cookie dough on 1 cookie ($1/2$ inch should be perfect for most, but hardcore cookie dough lovers may prefer to use more). Top with marshmallow and remaining cookie.

Note: Though cookie dough has a distinct flavor, it tends to get lost in s'mores, especially when combined with several other flavors. This recipe manages to isolate both the taste of the baked cookie and the dough. If you love cookie dough, this is a must-try s'more.

strawberry shortcake

2 yellow strawberry shortcake cups

Fresh sliced strawberries, to taste

1 marshmallow

Fill 1 shortcake cup with strawberry slices. Roast the marshmallow. Once marshmallow is done, slide it into remaining shortcake cup. Carefully invert the cup with marshmallow and place it atop the cup with strawberries.

bananas foster

4 banana slices

Cinnamon, to taste

Milk or dark chocolate, to taste

1 graham cracker, broken in half

1 marshmallow

Splash of rum (optional)

Sprinkle banana slices with cinnamon on both sides. Arrange chocolate on 1 of the graham cracker halves and melt. Roast the marshmallow. Once chocolate has melted, remove graham cracker from heat and add the bananas and roasted marshmallow. Quickly dip 1 flat side of the remaining graham cracker half in rum, if using, and top s'more.

Note: If you love burned marshmallows, try it with this recipe. Real bananas Foster always has flames.

mexican chocolate

Milk chocolate, to taste

1/2 graham cracker

1 marshmallow

1 soft snickerdoodle cookie

Cinnamon, to taste

Arrange chocolate on the graham cracker and melt. Roast the marshmallow. When the marshmallow is almost done, heat the cookie to soften. Once chocolate has melted, remove graham cracker from heat and sprinkle with cinnamon. Top with roasted marshmallow and cookie.

VARIATION For even more cinnamon flavor, use half of a cinnamon Pop-Tart instead of a snickerdoodle. But be careful, because Pop-Tarts fall apart when warm.

best brownies

Brownies are scrumptious in s'mores, and you can vary almost any recipe in this book by substituting a brownie for a top graham cracker. If you love brownies, be creative!

When working with brownies, keep a few things in mind. Brownies tend to be thick and very rich. If you sandwich two brownies together, you won't always be able to taste whatever you have enclosed in them. Instead, use a graham cracker on the bottom and a brownie on the top. The graham cracker also enables you to melt toppings more easily. If cooking with a lidded pan, you should be able to melt toppings on a brownie, but if you're cooking directly on a campfire or grill, your brownie might crumble into the fire or never get hot enough to melt any toppings. Finally, brownies have such a strong flavor that you don't always need a whole one to top your s'more; cut a smaller square and you'll still be delighted without overwhelming the other flavors you've chosen.

Oh, one more note: plain brownies work well, but these treats also come in many varieties and you can always use your favorite.

hazelnut raspberry brownie

1/2 graham cracker

Nutella, to taste

4 fresh raspberries

1 marshmallow

1 brownie square

Slather graham cracker generously with Nutella and then add raspberries, tapping to secure. Roast the marshmallow. Top graham cracker with roasted marshmallow and brownie square.

cookies 'n' cream brownie

1/4 full-size Hershey's Cookies 'n' Creme candy bar

1/2 graham cracker

1 marshmallow

1 brownie square

Arrange chocolate on the graham cracker and melt. Roast the marshmallow. Once the chocolate has melted, remove graham cracker from heat and top with roasted marshmallow and brownie.

minty brownie

1 marshmallow

A handful of Junior Mints

2 brownie squares or 1 brownie square and $1/2$ graham cracker

Roast the marshmallow. Place Junior Mints on 1 brownie square or graham cracker. Add roasted marshmallow and top with remaining brownie square.

Note: While all meltable mints are a s'more-lover's friend, Junior Mints work wonderfully with brownies because they are soft without melting, and their flavor is strong enough to complement even the most chocolatey brownie.

scotchy butterfinger brownie

Butterscotch chips, to taste

$1/2$ graham cracker

1 marshmallow

Small piece of Butterfinger bar, loosely chopped

1 brownie square

Arrange butterscotch chips on the graham cracker and melt. Roast the marshmallow. Once the butterscotch chips have melted, remove graham cracker from heat and sprinkle Butterfinger pieces over melted butterscotch. Top with roasted marshmallow and brownie square.

amy's lemon bar

White chocolate, to taste

1/2 graham cracker

Lemon curd, to taste

1 lemon cookie

1 marshmallow

Arrange chocolate on the graham cracker and melt. Spread a thin layer of lemon curd on the bottom of the lemon cookie and set aside. Roast the marshmallow. Once the chocolate has melted, remove graham cracker from heat and top with roasted marshmallow and cookie.

kettle corn

3 Hershey's Caramel Kisses, or any caramel-filled chocolate

1 graham cracker, broken in half

1 marshmallow

Salted and buttered popcorn, to taste

Arrange Kisses on 1 of the graham cracker halves and melt. Roast the marshmallow. Once Kisses look soft and shiny, remove graham cracker from heat and press pieces of popcorn into the melted chocolate and caramel. Top with roasted marshmallow and remaining graham cracker half.

piña colada

1 coconut cookie

Splash of rum (optional)

White, milk, or dark chocolate, to taste

$1/2$ graham cracker

1 marshmallow, preferably a Smashmallow Coconut Pineapple or Jet-Puffed Toasted Coconut

1 slice pineapple, about $1/2$ inch thick

Briefly dip the bottom side of the cookie in the rum, if using. Arrange chocolate on the graham cracker and melt. Roast the marshmallow. Once the chocolate has melted, remove graham cracker from heat. Top with pineapple slice, roasted marshmallow, and cookie.

VARIATION No cookies or special marshmallows on hand? Use coconut chocolate instead of plain, such as a Mounds bar, Lindt Excellence Coconut chocolate bar, or Lindt Excellence White Coconut chocolate bar.

biscotti latte

1 biscotto

$^1/_2$ graham cracker

Coffee-flavored
chocolate, to taste

Vanilla white chocolate,
chocolate with hazelnuts,
or Hershey's Caramel
Kiss, to taste

1 marshmallow

Break off a piece of biscotto about as long as the graham cracker and
set aside. Break chocolate selections into small pieces and arrange
on graham cracker (if you're using a Kiss, place in the middle of
graham cracker and arrange coffee-flavored chocolate around it). Melt
chocolate and roast the marshmallow. Once the chocolate has melted,
remove graham cracker from heat. If desired, stir chocolate slightly with
a toothpick or knife to mix. Top with roasted marshmallow and biscotto.

VARIATION For a dramatic, extra-large treat, use a full graham
cracker and unbroken biscotto.

coffee plus

Kahlúa, Irish cream, brandy, or libation of choice

Coffee-flavored chocolate, to taste

1 graham cracker, broken in half

1 marshmallow

Pour a bit of the Kahlúa into a saucer or small bowl and set aside. Arrange chocolate on 1 of the graham cracker halves and melt. Roast the marshmallow. Once the chocolate has melted, remove graham cracker from heat and slide marshmallow onto chocolate. Dip 1 flat side of the remaining graham cracker half into the Kahlúa to coat. Place graham cracker on top of roasted marshmallow, alcohol side down.

coffee talk

There are many varieties of coffee-flavored chocolate—almost every specialty chocolatier makes one—and some are stronger than others. When combining coffee-flavored chocolate with other flavored chocolates, such as in the Biscotti Latte recipe (page 62), be sure to taste them all before you begin so you can determine the right proportions for each. Ideally, you'll want to achieve a balance of the two flavors, which may require you to use more of one chocolate and less of another.

intense espresso

1 graham cracker,
broken in half

Nutella, chocolate spread, or a
chocolate candy bar of choice

1 marshmallow

6 chocolate-covered
espresso beans

Cover 1 of the graham cracker halves with a thin layer of Nutella, or melt a small amount of chocolate on the cracker and spread it evenly over the surface. Roast the marshmallow. Tap the espresso beans into the Nutella or melted chocolate to secure. Add roasted marshmallow and top with remaining graham cracker half.

Note: The chocolate layer in this s'more is there simply to cement the espresso beans, so Nutella or any sort of chocolate spread is the easiest option. You can also melt a thin layer of chocolate on the graham cracker half. Just don't use too much—you don't want to overpower the espresso flavor.

coffee toffee

Coffee-flavored
chocolate, to taste

$1/2$ graham cracker

1 marshmallow

1 toffee candy bar (such
as a Heath or Skor bar),
cut the same length as
the graham cracker

Arrange chocolate on the graham cracker and melt. Roast the
marshmallow. Once the chocolate has melted, remove graham cracker
from heat and slide the roasted marshmallow onto chocolate. Top with
the toffee bar.

german chocolate

1 Mounds candy bar, cut to fit on a graham cracker half

1 graham cracker, broken in half

1 marshmallow

Chopped pecans, to taste (optional)

Arrange the candy bar on 1 of the graham cracker halves and melt. Roast the marshmallow. Once the candy bar has melted, remove graham cracker from heat and add chopped pecans, if using. Top with marshmallow and remaining graham cracker half.

VARIATION If you like nuts but don't have pecans, swap a Mounds bar for an Almond Joy.

ilima's favorite fruit smoothie

Orange-flavored chocolate

1/2 graham cracker

1 marshmallow

Fruit slices and berries of your choice (strawberries, bananas, raspberries, mango, etc.), to taste

1 Pim's orange or raspberry biscuit

Arrange chocolate on the graham cracker and melt. Roast the marshmallow. When chocolate is soft, remove graham cracker from heat and add the fruit, tapping to secure in the melted chocolate. Add roasted marshmallow and top with the biscuit.

VARIATION This s'more is also delicious without chocolate. Stack up your fruit selections on the graham cracker with the most stable on the bottom. Roast the marshmallow. When the marshmallow is ready, add it to the fruit stack and top with the biscuit.

alexis' dirt and worms delight

Milk chocolate, to taste

2 chocolate cookies
or 1 chocolate graham
cracker, broken in half

1 marshmallow

2 gummy worms

Arrange chocolate on cookie or graham cracker half and melt. Roast the marshmallow. Once the chocolate has melted, remove cookie or graham cracker from heat. Add gummy worms to chocolate, making sure heads and tails are sticking out. Top with roasted marshmallow and cookie or remaining graham cracker half.

Note: Dirt and Worms is a kids' party treat usually made with chocolate pudding, cookie crumbles, and gummy worms. My eight-year-old loves this s'mores version. For those who see no reason to mix chocolate with gummy candies, adding a slice of strawberry makes the whole thing a bit more harmonious.

toasted coconut caramel

2 to 3 Hershey's Caramel Kisses, or any caramel-filled chocolate

1/2 graham cracker

1 Jet-Puffed Toasted Coconut marshmallow (hard to find but worth it)

1 Samoa or Caramel deLite Girl Scout cookie or similar cookie

Arrange Kisses on the graham cracker and place over heat. Roast the marshmallow. Once Kisses look soft or slightly melted, remove graham cracker from heat and top with roasted marshmallow. Finish with the cookie. This s'more will work with a regular marshmallow, but the toasted coconut variety is truly delicious.

Note: If it's not Girl Scout cookie season, you should be able to find Keebler Coconut Dreams in your local supermarket.

elevated tastes

strawberry balsamic

White chocolate, to taste

1 graham cracker,
broken in half

1 marshmallow

1 slice strawberry,
$1/2$–1 inch thick

Balsamic vinegar, to taste

Arrange chocolate on 1 of the graham cracker halves and melt. Roast the marshmallow. Once the chocolate has melted, remove graham cracker from heat and add strawberry slice and marshmallow. Pour a bit of balsamic vinegar into a small dish and dip one side of remaining graham cracker half in the vinegar until coated (the longer you leave it in, the more balsamic flavor you will get). Top s'more with the graham cracker, vinegar side down.

VARIATION For a fancier presentation, serve open faced with strawberry slices on top.

marzi-pear

2 to 4 squares marzipan-
filled chocolate

1 graham cracker,
broken in half

1 marshmallow

1 slice fresh, ripe pear,
about $1/2$ inch thick

Arrange marzipan chocolate on 1 of the graham cracker halves and melt. Roast the marshmallow. Once chocolate has melted, remove graham cracker from heat and add the pear slice. Top with roasted marshmallow and remaining graham cracker half.

maple bacon

Milk or dark chocolate, to taste

1 slice cooked bacon

1 graham cracker, broken in half

1 marshmallow

Maple syrup, to taste

Arrange chocolate on 1 of the graham cracker halves and melt. Break bacon into graham cracker-size pieces. Roast the marshmallow. Once the chocolate has melted, remove graham cracker from heat and add pieces of bacon. Drizzle with maple syrup. Top off with marshmallow and remaining graham cracker half.

sea salt caramel

2 Rolo candies

1 graham cracker, broken in half

1 marshmallow

Sea salt, to taste

Arrange candies on 1 of the graham cracker halves and melt. Roast the marshmallow. Once the chocolate has melted, remove graham cracker from heat and sprinkle chocolate with sea salt. Top off with remaining graham cracker half.

Note: I like the chewiness of the Rolo caramel in this recipe, but you can substitute any caramel-filled chocolate. Ghirardelli's Dark & Sea Salt Caramel chocolate squares are a decadent option.

the mint raspberry sophisticate

3 to 4 Andes mints

1 graham cracker,
broken in half

1 marshmallow

4 fresh raspberries

Arrange mints evenly on 1 of the graham cracker halves and melt. Roast the marshmallow. Once mints have melted, remove graham cracker from heat and add raspberries, lightly tapping to secure. Add roasted marshmallow and top with remaining graham cracker half.

s'blime

Lime-flavored
chocolate, to taste

1 graham cracker,
broken in half

1 marshmallow

1 tablespoon lime juice

1 tablespoon lime zest

Arrange chocolate on 1 of the graham cracker halves and melt. Roll marshmallow in lime juice (briefly—it will dissolve if left too long) and roast. Once the chocolate has melted, remove graham cracker from heat and sprinkle lime zest over chocolate. Add roasted marshmallow and top with remaining graham cracker half.

VARIATIONS You can use less lime and still have a tasty s'more. Lime-flavored chocolate alone is delicious, as is zest or juice with plain chocolate.

maria's lavender lift

Lavender-flavored chocolate, to taste

2 lavender cookies or 1 graham cracker, broken in half

1 marshmallow

Arrange chocolate on a cookie or graham cracker half and melt. Roast the marshmallow. Once the chocolate has melted, remove cookie or graham cracker from heat. Finish with roasted marshmallow and remaining cookie or graham cracker half.

VARIATION If you're using lavender cookies, you can substitute milk, white, or marzipan chocolate for the lavender chocolate.

Note: If you're lucky like me, you have a friend who grows her own lavender and bakes it into crispy cookies. If you're not so lucky, you can find lavender cookies at select farmers markets or specialty food stores. Baking your own is another option: add 1 tablespoon of ground culinary lavender to the creamed components (butter and sugar) of any basic sugar or butter cookie recipe. If that's too much hassle, lavender chocolate with good ol' graham crackers still tastes light and lovely.

spicy mayan chocolate

Dark chocolate, to taste

2 chocolate cookies or 1 cookie and 1/2 graham cracker

1 marshmallow

Cayenne pepper, to taste

Cinnamon, to taste (optional)

Arrange chocolate on cookie or graham cracker and melt. Roast the marshmallow. Once the chocolate has melted, remove cookie or graham cracker from heat. Sprinkle chocolate with cayenne pepper and cinnamon (if using), add marshmallow, and top with chocolate cookie.

Note: You can omit the cayenne and use pieces of a spicy chocolate bar instead.

sean's speculoos peach pie

Cookie butter*, to taste

1/2 graham cracker

1 slice peach, 1/2–1 inch thick

1 marshmallow

1 to 2 speculoos cookies*

Spread the cookie butter on graham cracker and top with peach slice. Roast the marshmallow. Top s'more with roasted marshmallow and 1 or 2 speculoos cookies.

*Speculoos (or speculaas) are European shortbread cookies that contain spices like cinnamon and ginger. Cookie butter is crushed and spreadable speculoos.

almond ginger melt

1 graham cracker,
broken in half

Almond butter, to taste

Dark chocolate, to taste

1 marshmallow

1 graham cracker-size piece
of dried candied ginger

Spread 1 of the graham cracker halves with almond butter and set aside. Arrange chocolate on remaining graham cracker and melt. Roast the marshmallow. Once the chocolate has melted, remove graham cracker from heat. Add ginger and roasted marshmallow. Top with the remaining graham cracker, almond butter side down.

Thanks to Bonnie Steward and Neva Healer for this recipe.

Note: You can find candied ginger in most natural food stores, sometimes pre-packaged, sometimes in the bulk bins. You can also purchase chocolate-covered ginger—equally good in this recipe—from many chocolatiers.

cinnamon chai

Chai-flavored
chocolate, to taste

1 graham cracker,
broken in half

1 marshmallow

Cinnamon, to taste

Arrange chocolate on 1 of the graham cracker halves and melt. Roast the marshmallow. Once the chocolate has melted, remove graham cracker from heat and sprinkle with cinnamon. Top with roasted marshmallow and remaining graham cracker half.

raspberry fig bar

2 dried figs, stems removed

4 fresh raspberries

1 graham cracker,
broken in half

1 marshmallow

Cut each fig into small pieces and cut each raspberry in half. Arrange fig pieces evenly on one of the graham cracker halves and then top with raspberries. Roast the marshmallow. Once marshmallow is roasted, slide it onto fruit and top with the remaining graham cracker half.

VARIATION Omit the dried figs and spread the bottom graham cracker with fig jam.

extreme variations

the peanut butter slob

2 full-size Reese's
Peanut Butter Cups

1 marshmallow

Unwrap peanut butter cups and set aside. Roast the marshmallow. Once marshmallow is roasted, sandwich it between the peanut butter cups. Eat quickly before it melts all over!

VARIATION For a version that's slightly less messy, use 1 Reese's Big Cup instead of 2 regular ones, sliding your marshmallow on top. Eat this variation like an open-faced sandwich. If you want, you can even scoop out some of the peanut butter filling and add another kind of candy, such as M&M's or chopped Butterfinger pieces.

emma's pound cake spectacular

2 slices pound cake, about $1/2$ inch thick

Nutella, to taste

Sliced strawberries, to taste

1 marshmallow

Generously cover 1 side of each pound cake slice with Nutella. Arrange strawberries over Nutella on 1 slice. Roast the marshmallow. Once marshmallow is roasted, place it atop the strawberries. Top with second pound cake slice, Nutella side down.

VARIATION For even more goodness, try toasting and buttering the pound cake before spreading it with Nutella.

stuffed apricot

1 apricot

Chocolate syrup, to taste

1 marshmallow

Chocolate chips or
chocolate slivers, to taste

Slice apricot in half along its natural seam and remove the pit.
Swirl a bit of chocolate syrup on each half of the apricot. Roast the
marshmallow, and then place on top of 1 apricot half. Poke chocolate
chips or slivers inside the hot roasted marshmallow and top with other
apricot half.

chocolate raspberry croissant

1 plain croissant

Dark chocolate, to taste

1 marshmallow

Fresh raspberries, to taste

Cut croissant in half lengthwise, making the bottom half thinner than the top half. Arrange chocolate on the bottom half of croissant and melt. The butter in the pastry will keep it from burning. Roast the marshmallow. Once the chocolate has melted, remove croissant from heat and tap raspberries into chocolate to secure. Finish with roasted marshmallow and the top half of the croissant.

black forest cupcake

1 chocolate cupcake,
unfrosted

1 to 2 fresh cherries,
pitted and sliced

Chocolate chips or
chocolate slivers, to taste

1 marshmallow

Scoop out a hole in your cupcake large enough to hold a roasted marshmallow (it's easiest just to pick out the cake and eat it). Place half of the cherry slices in the bottom of the cake cup and top with a few chocolate chips. Roast the marshmallow, ensuring it is heated through, and then add it to the cake cup. Insert chocolate into the hot roasted marshmallow, and top with the remaining cherry slices.

VARIATIONS Omit the chocolate chips and top the sliced cherries with hot fudge. Or, for an elegant presentation, slice the top off the cupcake, add the fillings, replace the cupcake top, and add a whole cherry, as shown in the photograph.

s'more parfait

Chocolate, caramel, or butterscotch syrup, to taste

1 ice cream cone (plain or sugar)

Candy or fruit of choice, chopped*, to taste

2 marshmallows

Drizzle syrup on the inside of ice cream cone to coat. Put a small amount of candy or fruit in the bottom of the cone. Roast the marshmallows. Once the marshmallows are roasted, insert 1 into the cone, using a knife or spoon to push the marshmallow as far into the cone as possible. Top with a second layer of candy or fruit. Add second roasted marshmallow and top with final layer of candy or fruit.

VARIATION For a giant-size parfait, use a waffle cone and create as many marshmallow/candy layers as you can. Flavored marshmallows work great!

Note: You can also convert almost every recipe in this book to parfait form simply by chopping and layering the ingredients in an ice cream cone.

*TRY THESE YUMMY FLAVOR COMBINATIONS
Oreo cookie pieces, chopped nuts, and sprinkles
Mixed berries and chocolate (all layers)
Dark chocolate, espresso beans, and chopped biscotti pieces
Chopped peaches, blueberries, and strawberries
Strawberries, Mounds bar, and pineapple
Chocolate with rice crisps, chocolate with nuts, and chocolate with cornflakes
Dark chocolate, milk chocolate, and white chocolate
Andes mint, Junior Mint, and Peppermint Pattie

banana nut muffin

1 banana nut muffin

4 banana slices

1 marshmallow

Milk or dark chocolate
with nuts, to taste

Separate the muffin top from the bottom. Create a cavity in the bottom part of the muffin and put 2 banana slices inside. Roast the marshmallow, ensuring it is heated through. Add marshmallow to the muffin bottom, and insert chocolate inside the hot marshmallow to melt. Complete sandwich with remaining banana slices and the muffin top.

VARIATIONS Use any muffin type you like and pair it with complementary toppings. Try blueberries and chocolate with a blueberry muffin, apples and caramel with an apple muffin, etc. The possibilities are endless.

the waffler

1 toaster waffle or homemade waffle, cut in half

1 marshmallow

Maple syrup, to taste

Heat waffle halves on the grill or in the toaster—the crispier, the better! Roast the marshmallow. Once the marshmallow is ready, slide it onto 1 of the waffle halves. Drizzle maple syrup over roasted marshmallow. Top with remaining waffle half and enjoy.

VARIATION Add your favorite fruit topping (such as cinnamon apples, berries, or bananas) to the bottom waffle before adding marshmallow and maple syrup. Or, for a savory twist, add a (boneless) piece of crispy chicken.

katy's krispy treat

1 Rice Krispies Treat

Nutella, to taste

Sliced strawberries, raspberries, or peaches, to taste (optional)

1 marshmallow

Slice Rice Krispies Treat in half lengthwise. Spread 1 of the halves with Nutella and top with fruit, if using. Roast the marshmallow. Once marshmallow is roasted, add it to the bottom slice and then top with remaining Rice Krispies Treat slice.

VARIATIONS If you don't have any Nutella handy or want to use regular chocolate, insert the chocolate into your marshmallow after you roast it. Do not attempt to melt on a Rice Krispies Treat—it will quickly melt or burn. For even more chocolate, go with a Cocoa Krispies Treat instead of the original.

hardcore mint

2 giant-size Peppermint Patties

1 marshmallow

Unwrap Peppermint Patties and set aside. Roast the marshmallow. Once the marshmallow is roasted, sandwich it between the Peppermint Patties. Eat quickly before it melts all over!

tracey's caramel apple

1 marshmallow

2 chewy caramels

2 green apple slices, about $1/2$ inch thick

Skewer marshmallow and 2 caramels on the same roasting stick, and then roast. When caramels have melted over the top of the marshmallow and the marshmallow is cooked to your liking, slide the concoction onto 1 of the apple slices. Top with remaining apple slice.

VARIATION Sprinkle top apple slice with cinnamon sugar.

stroopwafel taco

Hazelnut chocolate, preferably with hazelnut pieces, to taste

1 stroopwafel*, any flavor

1 marshmallow

Arrange chocolate on the stroopwafel and melt**. Roast the marshmallow. Once the chocolate has melted and stroopwafel is soft, remove stroopwafel from heat and slide the roasted marshmallow onto the melted chocolate. Fold stroopwafel in half and eat like a taco.

VARIATION This recipe is especially good with a crunchy chocolate. If you don't like nuts, try a chocolate containing rice crisps or cornflakes instead.

*A stroopwafel is a round Dutch wafer cookie with maple or honey filling inside. Ingeniously designed to rest atop a mug, the stroopwafel softens as the steam rises from the hot beverage within.

**Hot stroopwafels get droopy and difficult to handle, so it's best to heat them in a pan, not directly on a grill.

holiday favorites

sweetheart s'more

White chocolate, to taste

1 graham cracker,
broken in half

1 marshmallow

2 slices fresh strawberry

2 to 4 fresh raspberries

Arrange chocolate on 1 of the graham cracker halves and melt. Roast the marshmallow. Once the chocolate begins to melt, remove graham cracker from heat and top with berries, roasted marshmallow, and remaining graham cracker half.

shamrock s'more

3 to 4 Andes Mint Parfait Thins or green mint chips, to taste

2 chocolate cookies with green mint chips

1 marshmallow

Arrange mints on 1 cookie and melt. Roast the marshmallow. Warm second cookie to soften, if desired. Once the mints have melted, remove cookie from heat and top with roasted marshmallow and second cookie.

the squashed chickie

Milk chocolate, to taste (something from your Easter basket, if you like)

1 graham cracker, broken in half

1 marshmallow Peep, any color

Arrange chocolate on 1 of the graham cracker halves and melt. Skewer the Peep on a stick and heat very carefully—keep it farther away from the heat than you would a regular marshmallow. The sugar will instantly begin to heat and caramelize while the marshmallow filling liquifies. Remove Peep from heat and wait a few seconds; the cooling process will deliver a crispy outside shell for a nice crème brûlée effect. Once the chocolate has melted, remove graham cracker from heat and top with roasted Peep and remaining graham cracker half.

Note: Though we typically see the most of these marshmallow Peeps around Easter, the manufacturer also produces the same basic treats for other seasons and holidays.

the patriot

White, milk, or dark
chocolate, to taste

1 graham cracker,
broken in half

Fresh blueberries, to taste

1 marshmallow

1 thick strawberry slice,
or 2 to 3 smaller slices

Arrange chocolate on graham cracker half. Set blueberries atop
chocolate and melt, being careful not to lose the blueberries. Roast
the marshmallow. Once chocolate has melted, remove graham cracker
from heat and lightly tap blueberries to secure. Top with the strawberry
slice(s), roasted marshmallow, and remaining graham cracker half.

VARIATION For the most patriotic presentation, stack your
ingredients in red, white, and blue order. Just be careful not to lose
the strawberries when you take a bite.

smashing pumpkins

White chocolate, to taste

1 graham cracker, broken in half

1 marshmallow

Piece of pumpkin pie, cut to fit on graham cracker half*

Arrange chocolate on 1 of the graham cracker halves and melt. Roast the marshmallow. Once the chocolate has melted, remove graham cracker from heat and add pumpkin pie piece. Top with roasted marshmallow and remaining graham cracker.

VARIATION Omit the pumpkin pie and top your s'more with a pumpkin cookie instead.

*You can size your piece of pumpkin pie to suit your taste. For most, a slice 1 inch high should be perfect. Because pie is typically taller than that, I use a slice that's 1 inch wide and place it sideways on the graham cracker. However, for a more intense pumpkin flavor, you can use a taller piece of pie.

the saucy cranberry

White chocolate, to taste

1 graham cracker,
broken in half

1 marshmallow

Cranberry sauce (preferably
homemade), to taste

Arrange chocolate on 1 of the graham cracker halves and melt. Roast the marshmallow. Once the chocolate has melted, remove graham cracker from heat and spread a spoonful of cranberry sauce evenly over the top. Add roasted marshmallow and remaining graham cracker half.

candy cane

Milk chocolate (or any chocolate from your holiday festivities), to taste

1 graham cracker, broken in half

1 marshmallow

Candy cane pieces, loosely chopped, to taste

Arrange chocolate on graham cracker half and melt. Roast the marshmallow. Once the chocolate has melted, remove graham cracker from heat and lightly tap candy cane pieces in melted chocolate to secure. Add roasted marshmallow and top with remaining graham cracker half.

gingerbread house

1 marshmallow

2 gingerbread cookies, speculoos cookies, or slices of gingerbread

Assorted gumdrops, to taste

Roast the marshmallow. Remove it from heat and place it on 1 cookie or gingerbread slice. Wedge gumdrops in marshmallow and top with second cookie or gingerbread slice.

Note: Gingerbread is a strong flavor, so thinner cookies or gingerbread slices are better for this s'more. If your bread or cookies are too thick, try using a graham cracker in place of the bottom cookie or gingerbread slice.

resources

CHOCOLATES AND SPREADS

Some of the recipes in this book call for flavored chocolates not easily found in every candy aisle. This list of resources will help if you can't find your favorite flavor at your local specialty food store. You can also type in "specialty chocolate near me" in any internet search engine for endless possibilities!

Lindt
www.lindt.com
coconut, orange, lime, raspberry, toffee, blackberry, etc.

Ritter Sport
www.ritter-sport.de/en_US/
cornflake, marzipan, coconut, praline, macadamia, etc.

World Market
www.worldmarket.com
chai tea, banana, bacon, peanut butter, lavender, fig, etc.

Green & Black's
www.greenandblacks.com
vanilla white chocolate, mint, caramel, cherry, etc.

Chuao Chocolatier
www.chuaochocolatier.com
bacon, s'mores, potato chip, Spicy Maya, churro, honeycomb, etc.

Chocolove
www.chocolove.com
ginger, strawberry, chili, orange peel, etc.

Dagoba Organic Chocolate
www.dagobachocolate.com
lavender blueberry, ginger lime, raspberry mint, etc.

Nutella (Chocolate-hazelnut spread)
www.nutella.com

Speculoos cookie butter
www.biscoff.com
www.traderjoes.com

COOKIES

One of the best ways to spruce up a s'more is to replace the graham crackers with cookies. While some recipes call for specific, store-bought brands—such as Pim's biscuits and stroopwafels—many others call for basics such as chocolate chip cookies, sugar cookies, and snickerdoodles. When making those s'mores, you can use homemade cookies or purchase them at cookie shops or grocery stores. The key, wherever you get them, is to use soft, chewy cookies in your s'mores. If the cookies you have aren't fresh and soft, heat them up on the grill or stovetop or pop them in the microwave. And if you do have time, make homemade!

LU Biscuits (Pim's)
www.lubiscuits.com
Pim's biscuits, Petit Écolier, shortbread, and other elegant European cookies

www.stroopwafelshop.com
Dutch wafer cookies

MARSHMALLOWS

Add a specialty or gourmet marshmallow to your s'more for a new and tasty flavor combination.

www.smashmallow.com
a bunch of fun marshmallow flavors, available in major supermarkets and drug stores

www.plushpuffs.com
a huge variety of specialty marshmallow flavors

www.splitbeancoffee.com
specialty marshmallows, cookies, chocolates, coffees

index